Contents

Swimming

Competitors in a
100m breaststroke
race at the 2008
Paralympic Games
power through
the water.

Swimming is an important skill for everyone to learn. It
can be lots of fun on holiday or at your local pool.
Knowing how to swim can also save your life. You don't
have to take part in competitions to enjoy swimming,
but testing yourself against other swimmers in races
can be very exciting. You will need to be fit and fast to
be a winner!

Swimming races can take place over short distances
such as 50 metres, right up to races over many
kilometres. Swimmers forge their way through the
water using different swimming strokes. There are
four main strokes in swimming. These are front crawl,
back crawl, breaststroke and butterfly.

You don't need a lot of kit to take part in swimming races. All you need is a comfortable swimsuit that fits you well. If you have long hair, you can tuck it away under a swimming cap. It's a good idea to wear a tracksuit to keep you warm before and after swimming.

Another useful item is a good pair of goggles. These help you see clearly underwater. Always put the goggles over your eyes first and then pull the strap over your head.

▼ Holding swimming races with friends can be great fun. These young swimmers wear tops to keep warm before a race.

Tell me about...

Finishing first

A swimming race ends when all swimmers have swum the full distance and have touched the pool wall in front of them. Every swimmer aims to touch the wall first to win the race.

For most swimmers, the last part of the race is the hardest. Your body tires and it can be a struggle to keep on swimming smoothly. It is in this last part of the race that the strongest swimmers often move to the front.

▼ Rebecca Adlington wins the 400m freestyle at the 2008 Olympics. She timed her finish perfectly to beat the USA's Katie Hoff by just 0.07 of a second!

Many races are lost or won on a swimmer's final surge to the end of the pool. If you stretch out to reach the end of the pool too early, you may lose speed. If you wait too long, someone may touch the wall before you.

In big competitions, close finishes happen all the time. Special electronic touch pads are fitted to the pool walls. These are linked to a computer that works out the swimmers' times to hundredths or thousandths of a second. A giant screen displays these times after a race is over.

Do not get downhearted if you don't do well in a swimming race. Learn from any mistakes you made and work hard to swim faster next time.

Close finishes

Americans Nancy Hogshead and Carrie Steinseifer could not be separated at the 1984 Olympics. Their 100m race was the first official tie in Olympic history.

At the 2004 Olympics, the USA's Gary Hall Jr. beat Duje Draganja of Croatia in the 50m freestyle by 0.01 second! At the previous Olympics, Hall and his fellow American Anthony Ervin tied for the event and both won a gold medal.

▼ There are T-shaped markings on the pool floor. They let swimmers know that they are five metres away from the pool wall.

▼ A young swimmer touches the pool wall before his rivals to win the race.

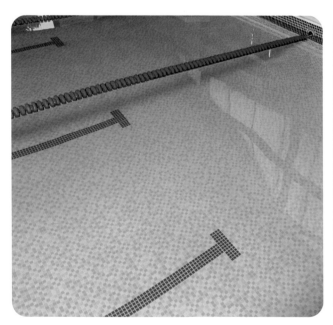

The pool

Some swimming races take place in the sea or in a lake. These are known as open water races. Most races, though, happen in a swimming pool.

Short course swimming events are held in a 25-metre-long pool. Long course swimming takes place in a 50-metre-long pool. Swimming at the Olympics is always in a 50-metre pool.

▼ A 25-metre swimming pool with the lanes marked out by floats called buoys. It may seem quiet now, but in a swimming gala it may be packed with fans.

▲ Many races are more than one length of the pool. Swimmers make special racing turns, somersaulting and pushing off the pool wall to begin their next length.

A competition swimming pool has certain special features. Just like a running track, the pool is divided up into eight lanes. The lanes are marked out on the pool floor and also by a string of floats on the top of the water. Swimmers must not leave their lane or they will be disqualified.

Most pools have a giant clock on the wall. They also have a

At the Olympics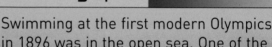

Swimming at the first modern Olympics in 1896 was in the open sea. One of the races was only for sailors from Greece.

The 1900 Olympics included a swimming obstacle race on the River Seine!

Open water swimming returned to the Olympics in 2008 with 10km races for both men and women.

line of flags that hang above both ends of the pool. These are five metres from each end of the pool. They help back crawl swimmers (see p20) judge how far they are from the pool wall.

Swimming stars

Champion swimmers like Michael Phelps and Ian Thorpe are big sports stars. They also train very, very hard. Each year, top swimmers spend thousands of hours in the pool in training, working with their coach. Many swim over 50,000 metres every week.

▼ US swimmer Dara Torres has some physiotherapy on her leg before a race. Top swimmers need to be in perfect condition to compete well.

Australian star swimmer Leisel Jones has ten pool sessions every week. She also works out in the gym twice a week and has two exercise bike sessions. Her training day begins when she gets up at 5.30 am!

Swimmers spend a lot of time stretching their muscles before training or racing. Stretching helps their bodies perform well and stops injuries. Swimmers also eat very healthily. They get advice on their diet from experts.

Most swimmers have to swim in more than one race during a competition. The first races are called heats and only the fastest swimmers from these heats qualify for the next round. As the swimmers take their places for the final race, the pressure is on. Top swimmers want to make all their training count.

▲ Michael Phelps (right) and Garrett Weber-Gale roar their approval as their team-mate in the 4 x 100m relay performs well at the 2008 Olympics.

Diving in

The back crawl and races for very young swimmers start in the water. Most races, though, start with the swimmers standing by the side of the pool on boxes called starting blocks.

An official called a starter controls the beginning of a race. On the starter's order, you climb onto your block. Your toes curl around the front of the block and you bend over, ready to spring.

▼ American swimmer Cullen Jones begins his dive in the 2007 World Championships 50m freestyle final. His arms will stretch forward and punch through the water.

▲ Swimmers are coiled up like a spring on their blocks. They are ready to make a fast, shallow dive into the water.

▲ Swimmers lift their hips and lower their head when they dive. They aim for their hands to punch a hole through the water. The rest of their body follows.

The starting signal can be a loud whistle blast or a bang from a starter's gun. When you hear the signal, you dive off the blocks into the water. You should try to glide along under the water as smoothly as possible.

Leaving your blocks early is called a false start. At big competitions, a swimmer who makes a false start is disqualified. If there has been a false start, a rope drops into the water ahead of the other swimmers to let them know.

▼ When gliding under the water, try to keep your arms and legs together. You want to be as narrow as possible. This helps you slice through the water.

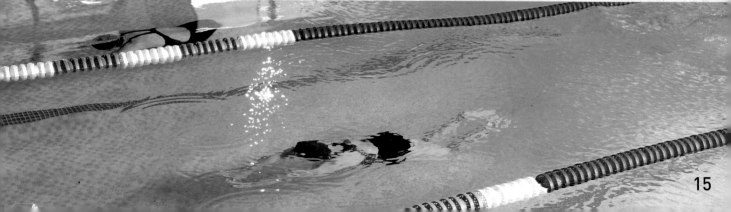

Freestyle

Freestyle means you can swim any type of stroke you like in a race. In fact, everyone chooses the front crawl in these races because it is the fastest stroke.

To swim the front crawl well, you need to get and keep your head in the water. Make your body as flat as possible with your legs stretched out behind you.

Your legs kick like a whip whilst your arms provide most of the power. Your hand, with fingers together, enters the water ahead of you. It presses back on the water.

▼ See how these swimmers do not make much of a splash as they swim. This is because their feet remain under the water and their hands enter the water cleanly. Big splashes mean wasted power.

Front crawl facts

American Johnny Weissmuller used the front crawl when he became the first person to swim 100m in less than a minute. He won five Olympic medals and later became famous as Tarzan in the movies.

South African Natalie Du Toit lost her left leg at the knee after a motor accident in 2001. She swims the front crawl without an artificial leg. In 2008, she managed to qualify to swim the 10km race at the Olympics.

◄

Your legs kick up and down under the water. Stretch your feet and point your toes as you kick.

Your arm travels back underwater. When it has passed your waist, it comes out of the water, elbow first. The arm then travels low through the air to begin its next stroke in front of your head.

The front crawl takes plenty of energy. Your legs kick all the time and one arm or the other is always in the water pushing it back. So, it's important to learn to pace yourself. Don't swim too fast at the start or you will run out of energy in the middle or end of a race.

►

Instead of lifting your head right up to breathe, you turn your head to one side. Part of your face stays in the water all the time.

Breaststroke

Breaststroke is thought to be the oldest of the main swimming strokes. You can swim breaststroke with your head up out of the water. But for a much faster version, used in races, you need to get your head under!

Make your body lie as flat as you can in the water. Your hips stay near the surface and your arms and legs stay in the water all the time.

▼ As your hands sweep under your chin, your head rises. This is when you take a breath before your head sinks under the water again. From this position, your arms stretch out in front of you again.

Move your arms out in front of you so that you are long and stretched. Then, sweep both hands out and round so that they end up almost below your chin. Your arms make a heart-shaped pattern under the water.

Look at the sequence of photos at the bottom of this page. As your arms move, your feet kick in a sort of circle as well. Both feet move at the same time.

In races, breaststroke is the slowest of the strokes, but is still powerful if swum well. In a breaststroke race, both hands have to touch the pool wall at the same time when making a turn or finishing the race.

▼ Your knees bend and your feet are brought up towards your bottom.

▼ Your feet point out towards either side.

▼ Your legs go straight again with your knees just touching.

Back crawl

The backstroke or back crawl is the only one of the four main strokes where your face isn't in the water. It is also the only one where you start a race already in the water.

At a major race, the pool wall has special bars for swimmers to hold. You pull yourself up into a coiled position with your head tucked in. If there are no bars, you grip the edge of the pool.

On the starter's whistle or pistol, you fling your arms back and push off really hard with both feet. You push your stomach up to arch your back. Your hands, then your arms, are the first parts of your body to enter the water.

▼ Swimmers start a back crawl race. Although their bodies rise out of the water on the start, their feet must remain in the water.

The back crawl movement is similar to the front crawl. Your legs kick up and down from the hips. One arms travels through the air whilst the other one sweeps and pulls through the water. A common mistake is to let your bottom drop low. Try to keep your body nice and flat and most of your head under the water.

▲ See how narrow the swimmer looks. This is called being streamlined. A streamlined shape allows you to cut through the water faster.

▼ This swimmer's right arm travels high through the air. His head faces the ceiling and stays as still as possible.

Back crawl facts

Hungary's Krisztina Egerszegi became the youngest Olympic swimming champion in 1988. Aged 14 she won the 200m backstroke.

In 2007, Aaron Piersol of the USA became the first person to swim the 100m backstroke in less than 53 seconds.

Butterfly

▲ France's Malia Metella swims the butterfly during the 2006 European Swimming Championships. Her body stays symmetrical throughout her swim.

Invented about 60 years ago, the butterfly is the newest stroke in swimming races. It is also the most spectacular. Swimmers surge forward with their arms coming out of the water.

You need to be fit and a good swimmer to swim the butterfly. It is probably the last of the main strokes you will learn. It is best to practise it in short bursts of action.

Both arms work together. Your elbows leave the water first and then your arms pass low over the water. They stay about shoulder-width apart as they enter the water ahead of you. As they pass back underneath your body, your head rises and you can take a breath.

While your arms are making this strong movement, your legs are moving, too. Both legs perform the same movement at the same time. They stay close together and travel up and down together. This type of movement is called the dolphin kick.

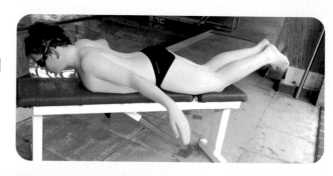

▲ See how the head rises just enough for you to take a breath.

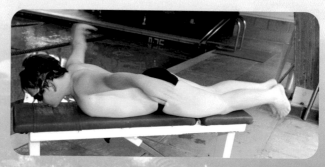

▲ Your legs are moving up and down together with your feet stretched.

▲ Once in the water, your arms sweep outwards and then inwards.

▼ Michael Phelps cuts through the water as his head rises to take a breath. Top swimmers often only breathe every second stroke.

Relays and medleys

Relay races are for teams of four swimmers. All four swimmers swim the same distance. At the Olympics, there are two relay events with each swimmer swimming 100m or 200m. These are called the 4 x 100m and the 4 x 200m.

One swimmer starts and swims his or her distance while the next swimmer gets on the starting block and waits. He or she can only dive in once the team-mate touches the pool wall. Relay swimmers swim front crawl throughout the race. Some teams put their strongest swimmer on the last leg of the relay to make up any lost time.

▼ Swimmers in a relay race get ready to take over from their team-mates.

Relays and records

The USA's Gertrude Ederle won a gold medal in the 4 x 100m relay at the 1924 Olympics. In 1926 she became the first woman to swim the English Channel.

Stephanie Rice of Australia broke the 400m Individual Medley world record in 2008. Three days later, she broke the 200m Individual Medley world record as well.

In medley races swimmers use all four of the main strokes. Some medley races are relays, with a team of four swimmers. Each swimmer swims one of the strokes. Individual medleys are really tough races. You have to swim each of the four strokes yourself. You start with butterfly, then back crawl and breaststroke. You finish with front crawl.

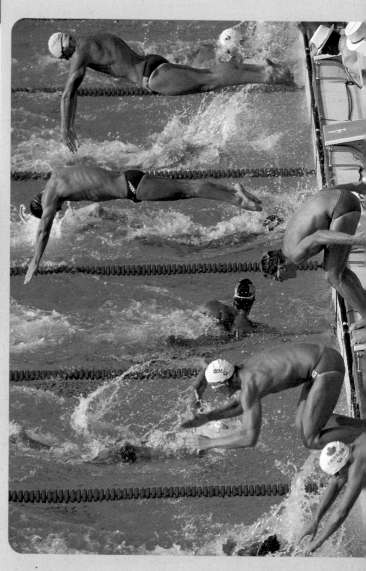

▲ Relay and medley teams support each other and train together.

▶

The changeover in a relay race can be hard to follow. Officials watch each lane, checking to see that the changeover between swimmers is correct.

The world of swimming

The greatest swimming competition is at the Olympic Games. Every four years, thousands of fans pack into an Olympic aquatic centre to watch the wide range of swimming races. Millions more cheer on their favourite swimmers at home on TV.

▼The 2004 Olympics 200m men's freestyle final begins. This famous race saw Australia's Ian Thorpe (lane 5) beat Pieter van den Hoogenband of the Netherlands (lane 4) and the USA's Michael Phelps (lane 3).

Competition is really strong at the Olympics. The two leading countries are Australia and the USA. Other nations such as the Netherlands, Russia, Germany and the UK also do well at the Olympics. To get into a country's Olympic team, swimmers have to win races called trials or do well in their national swimming championship.

The next biggest event is the World Aquatic Championships. It is held every two years with the 2009 competition in Rome, Italy. Diving and water polo sports are also included as well as lots of swimming events.

During the 2007 championships in Australia, 15 world records were broken, five by American swimmer, Michael Phelps!

A world championships for short course swimming in a 25m pool is also held every two years. The last was in Manchester, England, and in 2012 the competition will take place in Dubai.

Great champions

In 1972, American Mark Spitz won an incredible seven Olympic gold medals in swimming.

At the 2008 Olympics, Michael Phelps broke Spitz's amazing record. He won eight gold medals.

The USA's Natalie Coughlan has won more World Championship swimming medals than any other woman. She has six gold, six silver and four bronze medals.

▼ Australia's Liesel Jones powers down her lane during a heat for the 2008 Olympics 200m breaststroke. Jones won a silver medal in this event to go with her career total of three Olympic and seven World Championship gold medals.

Where next?

These websites and books will help you to find out more about swimming.

Websites

http://www.fina.org

This is the website of FINA, the organisation that runs world swimming. You can read all about the top swimmers and competitions.

http://www.pullbuoy.co.uk/

This website has news and features about competitive swimming worldwide.

http://www.totalimmersion.net/

This American website offers a monthly swimming magazine and great video lessons that are free to download.

http://www.usaswimming.org/

There is information about top American swimmers as well as swimming and training tips at this website.

http://www.britishswimming.org/

Thousands of people learn to swim or improve their swimming using coaching guides or awards offered by the Amateur Swimming Association. Learn more at their website.

Books

A World-class Swimmer by Paul Mason (Heinemann Library, 2004)
A description of how swimming champions train and compete.

Know Your Sport: Swimming by Paul Mason (Franklin Watts, 2008)
Information about all the different swimming strokes and competitive events.

Swimming words

deck the area around the swimming pool reserved for swimmers, officials and coaches

disqualified removed from a swimming race for breaking a rule

false start an error made by a swimmer who enters the pool or starts a race before the starter has given the signal

flexibility being able to bend easily

glide move smoothly through the water without moving your arms and legs

heat an early race in an event. The fastest swimmers in a heat enter the semi-finals or final

individual medley a race in which you swim an equal distance using all four swimming strokes

medley relay a relay race where each swimmer swims a different stroke

professional someone who is paid to swim

relay a race for teams of swimmers, with four people in each team. Swimmers take it in turns to swim their distance

starting blocks raised platforms for swimmers to stand on at the start of many races

tie when two swimmers finish a race at exactly the same time

Index

Numbers in **bold** refer to pictures.